va/a)

Yellow Umbrella Books are published by Capstone Press
151 Good Counsel Drive, P.O. Box 669, Mankato, Minnesota 56002
www.capstonepress.com

Library of Congress Cataloging-in-Publication Data
Cipriano, Jeri S.
    At the park / by Jeri Cipriano.
    p. cm.
    Summary: Simple text and photographs present the many different things people can do in parks.
    ISBN 0-7368-2907-5 (hardcover)—ISBN 0-7368-2866-4 (softcover)
    1. Parks—Juvenile literature. 2. Parks—Recreational use—Juvenile literature.
[1. Parks.] I. Title.
SB481.3.C55 2004
333.78'3—dc21   2003007742

Editorial Credits
Editorial Director: Mary Lindeen
Editor: Jennifer VanVoorst
Photo Researcher: Wanda Winch
Developer: Raindrop Publishing

Photo Credits
Cover: Photodisc/PhotoDisc; Title Page: DigitalVision; Page 2: Comstock; Page 3: PhotoDisc; Page 4: Photodisc/PhotoDisc; Page 5: Corel; Page 6: Royalty-Free/Corbis; Page 7: Michael S. Yamashita/Corbis; Page 8: Kevin Fleming/Corbis; Page 9: Photodisc/PhotoDisc; Page 10: Phil Lando/Image Ideas, Inc.; Page 11: EyeWire; Page 12: Photodisc/PhotoDisc; Page 13: Elizabeth Hathon/Corbis; Page 14: Royalty-Free/Corbis; Page 15: Doug Menuez/PhotoDisc; Page 16: Royalty-Free/Corbis

1 2 3 4 5 6 09 08 07 06 05 04

At the Park

by Jeri Cipriano

Consultant: Dwight Herold, EdD, Past President,
Iowa Council for the Social Studies

Yellow Umbrella Books

an imprint of Capstone Press
Mankato, Minnesota

Let's go to the park!

We can play ball in the park.

Some parks have lakes. We can feed the ducks that swim there.

We can watch people row.

Some parks have special paths for walking.

We might see some squirrels along the way.

Some parks have petting zoos.
We can pet the animals.

Some parks have gardens.
We can smell the flowers.

Some parks have rides.
We can ride horses that
go around and around.

Some parks have playgrounds.
We can swing high in the air!

Some parks have places for picnics. We can bring food from home.

We can buy food to eat.

Some parks have places to sleep.
We can sleep in a tent.

14

Let's have fun at the park.

Parks are for people!

Words to Know/Index

Word Count: 127
Early-Intervention Level: 9

17